Enneagram exercises
for personal growth

Enneagram Type 1
The Reformer

Created by Youaremoreworld

Enneagram exercises for personal growth: The Reformer
Created by Youaremoreworld

Copyright ©Youaremoreworld

For more information visit us: www.youaremoreworld.com or contact via email:
youaremoreworld@gmail.com

The names of the people in this book have been changed in order to protect their privacy.

The text was written by Viltare Veckyte based on the knowledge of Enneagram.

Graphics designed by: Simona Pozyte

First printed on Amazon, 2021.

ISBN 9798701570007

I welcome you on the journey of self discovery

agree to do daily exercises which will lead me to my personal growth. I do this because I see the importance of releasing my old habits and taking full responsibility for creating the life I want to live. I want to grow and explore my potential.

I will be true to myself by following daily practices which will encourage self-empowerment and personal appreciation. From today onward, personal growth will be one of my highest priorities in every day, and I promise to spend at least 10 minutes a day doing something which supports my true self.

_____   _____
Signature   Date

Introduction

Dear reader,

This Enneagram exercise book is a valuable tool which can guide you along your spiritual journey, helping you to grow and expand to your true nature. The material is intended to support those who already have some understanding of the Enneagram and are most likely also familiar with their own personality type. It will support these readers to go deeper by unraveling behavioural patterns and releasing blocks which may be preventing them from experiencing their full potential.

If you are unfamiliar with Enneagram and uncertain of your Enneagram type, a great place to start is to take an Enneagram Personality Test. This test along with other helpful information can be found at **www.youaremoreworld.com**.

The book opens with a foreword from the author, as she addresses all those who share your type, reminding you that you are not alone in the concerns which you experience. In the following pages you will be guided to discover more about your type from the basis of the behavioral patterns which are common for your personality type; exploring what you like, what is important to you and also what is essential in order for you to maintain balance in your day-to-day life. There are many thoughts which are valuable for you to bring awareness to which can help you to find greater connection with yourself.

The introductory Enneagram theory was left out of this book, as there are many valuable and in-depth sources where this can be explored. The aim of this book is to bring a fresh perspective to Enneagram, through working with habitual personality patterns, discovering greater understanding of personality traits and releasing false stories through daily practices. The resulting goal is to support you in your daily experiences and to guide you into the full integration of you with your wholeness.
Within this book you will find some daily practices from well know Enneagram teachers, as well as practices which have been tailored specifically for your personality type. By applying these practices daily you will experience the greatest benefit, gaining a better understanding of yourself, your preferences and your relationships. Through this work on the exercises you will experience the freedom which has always been a part of you, increasing your self-esteem and unraveling your unique gifts and strengths.

This book offers you the path to the truth which will free you to your wholeness.

Author's note

Thank you for trusting in me to guide you to explore your inner world.

We could all agree that life can be considered a journey, filled with ups and downs; joys and sadness. All of these moments arrive and then fade away, and all the while we remain observers to the experience simply noticing these changes as they occur. As we travel on this journey, we all reach moments when we begin to question ourselves, looking for new ways to change the course of our lives. In moments like these we are drawn to look within our own hearts and truly meet ourselves, sometimes for the very first time.

This Enneagram exercise book was created for this purpose of discovering greater inner awareness, offering guidance for you who have recognised that you hold dominant qualities of "The Reformer". It will support you and remind you that you are not alone on this journey; that many of us have similar questions and are also seeking a deeper connection to ourselves.

This book will also provide a blueprint for greater personal understanding and the support to unfold all of the qualities which you hold within, to truly flourish within your experience of life. It will remind you that there is no better path to personal growth than simply laying out all of our qualities in plain sight; seeing them as they are and recognising the value that each one of them brings us.

The information contained within this book can hold tremendous power for personal change and by exploring this book you may also experience some changes within yourself. When faced with this new information and the resulting changes, your willingness to remain open can allow you to discover more about yourself, and your experience of life, than you might expect.

As you turn the page you will be taking your first step on this new journey.

Are you ready?

How to use this book

This book is made up of four parts: Discovering Myself, Revealing Myself, Accepting Myself and Healing Myself. Although it can be tempting to skip ahead, we recommend using this book in the order in which it is laid out, as each chapter can provide a greater depth of understanding and when followed as recommended, has the potential to create powerful changes in your life.

Chapter　– **"Discovering Myself"** – This chapter explores many aspects of your dominant type, bringing you greater awareness of your personal traits. This exploration allows you to determine if this is truly your dominant type and to see yourself from an open and understanding perspective, to better understand the basis of this dominant Enneagram type. You will also learn to recognize your personal traits, your gifts and the challenges you face related to having this dominant type.

Chapter　– **"Revealing Myself"** – This chapter leads you through 40 exercises which have been created specifically for your dominant type. These exercises will expand your understanding of situations you face and also awaken a deeper connection with yourself through awareness of your daily behaviors. It is very important that you complete each of the exercises as they each have a meaningful message which can only be explored through personal experience. You will find that there is also great value in writing your thoughts and observations as well as the feelings you experience as you go, as this can develop a deeper connection within yourself.

Chapter　– **"Accepting Myself"** – This chapter will provide you with a greater sense of acceptance of who you are. Having explored the dominant qualities of your Enneagram type and some of the repetitive situations you find yourself falling into, you might begin to feel more aware of who you are in the present moment. You may still feel some hesitation about some of your qualities, but allowing yourself to practice acceptance of who you are in this moment will allow you to experience a greater sense of freedom of who you can be. You will discover how you can apply this self-acceptance to your own life. Only when we accept the qualities, we do not like about ourselves do we gain the freedom to choose how we really want to be.

Chapter　– **"Healing Myself"** – Each of us has many qualities that were formed in order to protect us. As we grow and develop, we begin to recognize some of them as qualities we do not really like but we feel powerless to change them. First, through our awareness we can notice them, then through acceptance we bring them out of the shadows, and finally through healing we can lovingly change and release them. In this section you will find carefully selected practices that can help you to observe and connect with these qualities in greater depth, which when practiced daily, can cause a very big shift in your life.

Discovering myself

Insightful questionnaire

Type description

Childhood message

How to get along with you

Famous people who share your type

Personal stories shared by others of your type

Before we start, mark the qualities that resonate with you

This section was created to determine whether this workbook is best suited to your dominant Enneagram type.

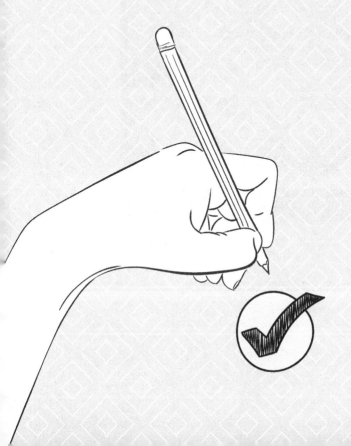

○ I like taking **responsibility.**

○ I constantly experience a sense of **having a "mission".**

○ I always **follow through on agreements.**

○ I have a **strong inner critic** which controls my thoughts, words, and actions.

○ I try to be **perfect** and I feel a responsibility that everything should be **done in the right way.**

○ My focus is on being a **good person.**

○ I often say **no to pleasures;** to me, they are of lesser importance.

○ I become **angry** when someone does not follow rules and standards.

○ It is important to me that everyone is **treated equally.**

○ I tend to **keep my anger** to myself.

○ I am afraid to **make mistakes.**

○ I am **impatient.**

○ I help others to **improve their lives.**

○ I feel **tension inside.** Sometimes I lash out at others.

○ I tend to **control my emotions** and personal needs.

○ I constantly feel like I need to **improve the environment** around me.

○ It is **hard** for me **to relax.**

○ I have very **high standards** for myself and my surroundings.

○ **Competence and honesty** are important to me.

○ I want to be **right.**

○ I **judge others** for their imperfections and non-compliance with standards.

○ It is hard for me to **say no.**

○ I am **principled.**

○ I have high standards and adhere to etiquette. I apply this approach in everything I do.

○ It is hard for me **to be alone.**

○ I have a very good eye for **small details.**

○ I see things as either **right or wrong, good or bad.**

○ I try to **be good,** even if I need to give up my true feelings or opinions.

○ It is important to me to be **appreciated and praised.**

○ I ask a lot of myself.

○ It is difficult for me **to express my feelings.**

○ I always follow the **rules and standards.**

○ I often feel overwhelmed by the **amount of responsibilities** I take on.

○ No matter what I do I often feel that it is **not good enough.**

○ I often experience **anger** when others don't put as much effort as I do, into work, relationships, etc.

MY RESULT:

 _____ /**35**

If you ticked **more than 25 out of 35,** you are most likely a Type 1 — also called "The Reformer" — and we welcome you to continue your journey. In the following pages you will discover a deeper understanding of yourself along with the tools and support you need to experience your inner authenticity.

If you ticked **fewer than 25,** we recommend that you read more about Types 3, 6 and 8, which are the most common mistyped personalities for Type 1.

The

RE FOR MER

People of this type typically believe that they have to **be good** and **do what is right** in order to be loved by others. They have imagined ideals which they try to live up to, and help others to do the same. They hold the intention for everybody to become closer to **perfection.** They feel inside that they **have a "mission",** which makes them always want to improve their life and the lives of others.

For the Reformer, **idealism** wakes up their energy and motivates them to work hard and live up to created **standards.** Their faith and belief in perfection divides the world which they experience into that which meets their ideals and that which doesn't. In other words, divided into **good and bad, right and wrong.** It is from here that they find the inspiration to **improve** their surroundings, in order for them to become closer to the ideals in their head.

Your true nature:

To see perfection within yourself and the wider world, as it already is in this present moment.

The most important mission for
me is to **discover my natural state of integrity,**
and **rest in my inherent inner goodness.**

In focusing all of their effort toward this **constant improvement,** they can experience anger toward others who are not doing the same.

People who belong to this type tend to compare reality with how it is "supposed to be," and have difficulty accepting it as it is. Their **inner critic** puts them in a state of judgment, which promotes a sense of inadequacy. By living with this outward-facing, judgment-based focus, they do not allow any space to care for themselves and their true needs. This leads them on the endless journey of becoming a **"good and right"** human being.

This "right and wrong" understanding of the world doesn't allow the Reformer to experience negative emotions. They deem emotions such as **anger** to be wrong—afraid to express this, as they imagine they will be seen as "bad people." This results in **suppression of these "bad" emotions,** often held just beneath the surface.

When the Reformer can release the belief that **love and validation** only come if you are good and **following the rules,** they begin to bring a valuable view which is **ethical and honest.** They start to understand that there is more than one right way to live, and they accept feelings of "not enough" and inadequacy in themselves and others.

The Reformer can have very **high standards,** and these can drive them to realize **something bigger.** Their personal journey starts when they question what they **really want,** rather than just acting in the way that is **"right."**

The anger within you often manifests itself on the outside as dissatisfaction and guilt for everything that turns out to be wrong or does not meet your high standards. People of your type are constantly trying to avoid mistakes, often falling into behaviors which are contrary to how they feel inside. An example would be behaving very friendly with people they don't like because they feel it is right to do so. (This pattern of behavior is automatic, done without even thinking.)

What is important to you:

◇   To do things in the right way

◇   To improve things so that they will meet my standards

◇   To not make mistakes and to avoid criticism

◇   Follow through on my responsibilities

◇   To be organized

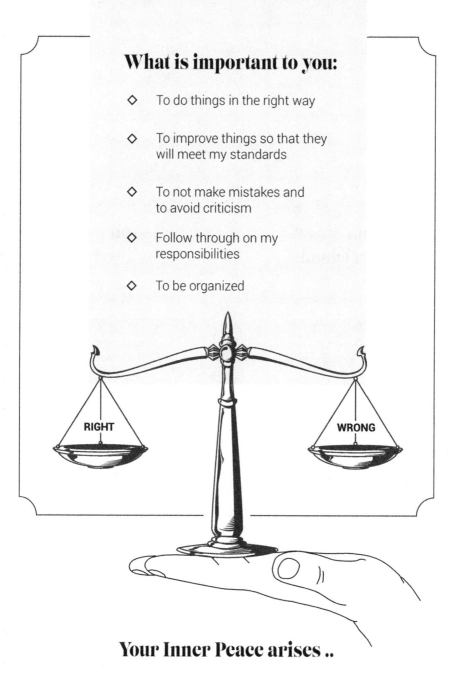

Your Inner Peace arises ..

*when you **change your relationship with anger** and **accept mistakes** as a natural part of learning and growth. You can begin to relax as your focus shifts from making mistakes or correcting differences to instead pursuing your natural desires.*

You do not feel good:

When you are not good
enough, not right or
see yourself as a bad
person.

You believe:

That you are good and
accepted when you do
what is right.

It is important to you:

To improve your surroundings,
follow the rules, and do
the right thing.

I wish for you:

To change what you can
change and accept what you
cannot change. To expand your
inner wisdom by seeing the
difference between the two.

What I like about my type:

- ◈ **Inner discipline** and the ability to achieve set goals.
- ◈ Ability to work hard to **improve the world.**
- ◈ Possession of **high inner-standards.**
- ◈ Being **responsible, smart** and **dedicated** to everything I do.
- ◈ Ability to combine all available information and make **effective decisions** as a result.
- ◈ Being able to be **the best I can be** and to draw out the best qualities of others.
- ◈ Being independent and being able to **get a lot of work done.**

The Message from Childhood

The knowledge of Enneagram gives us an explanation of how our personalities have been formed. This formation starts from a very early age and in Enneagram is referred to as **"the message we received in childhood"**.

We came into this world to express our full potential. In the first stages of our life, we do not have any personal conclusions about the world, for example what is „good" or what is „bad". From the moment we are born our mind is already actively observing our surroundings and with every interaction it forms an understanding of the world. During this very vulnerable stage of our development **our parents play a significant role.** We are instinctively wired for belonging to them and they become our whole world during this period of life. As we observe their behavior and day-to-day responses, we form our understanding of the world around us.

However, at this stage we do not have much experience with which to compare and we collect many false messages, conclusions which might be reached from having just one bad experience. For example: your parents may not have wanted to play with you and did not explain why, so you might have come to your own conclusion about why they do not want to play with you. Or perhaps you were in the hospital and your mother could not come to visit you on time because of problems at her work and you might have come to the conclusion that you need to take care of yourself because no one else will. **Take a good look at the messages** written on the following page, **allow yourself to stay with them** observing what they bring to you. If it is difficult for you to find meaning in the messages this is totally natural, simply take further steps to explore more about your type and occasionally return to these messages to see if they bring more meaning to you.

Misunderstood message

The message we received in childhood and understood as truth, basing our further life experience on.

"It is not okay to make mistakes."

Core fear

The inner fear that triggers us to build certain qualities in order to protect ourselves.

"I am afraid to be bad, evil or defective."

Lost message

The supportive message we were craving from others, but never received.

"It is not true - you are good as you are."

—⟨◇⟩—

Authenticity is the daily practice of letting go of who we think we're supposed to be and embracing who we are.

Brené Brown

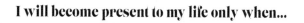

I will become present to my life only when...

———⟨ ◇ ⟩———

*I have attained complete balance and integrity, make no
mistakes and have everything in my world sensibly organized.
When I have achieved perfection, then I'll show up.*[4]

What other people of your type say about themselves

Enneagram knowledge helps us to see that some of our behavioral patterns, preferences and views about the world are shared with others who belong to the same dominant Enneagram type as us. This can give us comfort in the knowledge that we are not alone on this journey and we can always find someone who understands us in greater depth. Take a good look at the following sentences shared by people of your type.

⟨ ◈ ⟩

◇ I always **follow my word.** If I say I will do it, I always keep promise.

◇ I have a **strong critic inside,** which controls my thoughts, words, and things I do.

◇ I try to be perfect, and feel very responsible for everything being done in the **right way.**

◇ I become **angry when someone does not follow rules** and standards.

◇ I am afraid to **make mistakes.**

◇ I usually **say what I think.**

◇ I have **ideals in my head** and try to live up to them.

◇ **Honesty** is important for me.

◇ It is very common for me to **control my emotions** and personal needs.

◇ I value everything as **right or not right, good or bad;** there is no middle-ground for me.

How to get along with me

We can build deeper understanding in our relationships by sharing what is important to us. Through sharing our preferences, others will understand us more intimately, often resulting in them offering greater support to us. In turn this gives us more opportunities to offer the same support to others.

Below are some key qualities which, when respected, provide those of our type a supportive basis to be the best they can be.

⟨ ◈ ⟩

1. Help me by sharing responsibilities and take care of the things which you are responsible for.

2. Praise my achievements and evaluate what I do.

3. I always ask a lot of myself. Please remind me that I am good enough as I am.

4. Apologize if you don't act in the right way. That will help me to forgive you.

5. Help me to laugh at myself, but please don't discredit my worries.

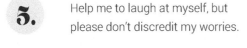

◇

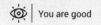

Famous people like you

The best teachers are the ones who have walked a similar path ahead of us. Their examples can give us hope, inspiration and guidance on where we can take our own paths and how our qualities can empower us on this journey.

The Enneagram Institute has compiled a very comprehensive list of well-known people who share the same dominant Enneagram type as you. Take some time to explore the lives of the people listed below and you may discover what a valuable resource it can be for your own development.

Confucius, Plato, Salahuddin Ayyubi, Joan of Arc, Sir Thomas More, Mahatma Gandhi, Pope John Paul II, Nelson Mandela, Margaret Thatcher, Prince Charles, Kate Middleton, Duchess of Cambridge, Jimmy Carter, Michelle Obama, Al Gore, Hilary Clinton, Rudy Giuliani, Elliot Spitzer, Justice Sandra Day O'Connor, Osama bin Laden, George Bernard Shaw, Thoreau, Dr. Jack Kevorkian, Anita Roddick (The Body Shop), Martha Stewart, Chef Thomas Keller, Michio Kushi (macrobiotics), George Harrison, Joan Baez, Celine Dion, Ralph Nader, Noam Chomsky, Bill Moyers, George F. Will, William F. Buckley, Keith Olbermann, Jerry Seinfeld, Bill Maher, Tina Fey, Katherine Hepburn, Maggie Smith, Emma Thompson, Julie Andrews, Vanessa Redgrave, Jane Fonda, Meryl Streep, Harrison Ford, Helen Hunt, Captain "Sully" Sullenberger, "Mary Poppins," "Mr. Spock," SNL's "The Church Lady".

(Source: www.enneagraminstitute.com)

“Freedom is not
worth having
if it does not include
the freedom to
make mistakes.”

Mahatma Gandhi

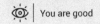

**At your best you
open up and become:**

—⟨ ◈ ⟩—

Idealistic Reliable Ethical Tidy Productive Purposeful Wise

When you do not feel balanced
you tend to:

—⟨◇⟩—

Critical Inflexible
Self- righteous
Controlling
Judgmental
Angry

People of your type shared some stories from their life

—⟨◈⟩—

As a child, I learned that there is only one right way of doing things in life, and that is my dad's way. Sometimes he changed his way; he was inconsistent. But his way has always been 'right.' In response to my father's inconsistent behavior, I decided to look for the 'right' way in life and in the world.

— Edmund, 49.

In our family, while I was growing up, there was always an intense atmosphere. Every day ended in some kind of conflict. Whenever a conflict would arise I felt inside that I had to prevent it or fix it in some way. It probably had some influence on my controlling nature. My mother was very aggressive, and to protect myself I also identified with that anger and took it as a quality. I grew up very critical, judgmental, and stubborn. I treated my sister the way my mother treated us. I was very domineering and demanding.

— Carla, 33.

Yes, there are personalities who I idolize as living in the right way. For a long time they inspired my way of living, and I tried to help others get closer to their perfection as well. I got all sorts of reactions from those around me as I tried to help them. Sometimes they thanked me, but most of the time I was either ignored or met by remarks like, 'Please don't tell me what to do.' I was outraged. What do you mean 'don't tell me what to do'? I am just trying to help you. It wasn't until many years later that I considered; what if others didn't want me to help them? And what if they have other ideals that have completely opposite values? And in general, do I really know what is 'better'? I still have a lot of open questions, but I have learned one thing: to not push my own truths on others; and only when someone asks, to share my advice.

- Martin, 49.

I have learned that I become irritable when my needs are not met right here and now. These can be very simple needs such as hunger, or more complex ones such as an unresolved conflict with a colleague. I am practicing not blaming myself for being so quickly affected, but it's better to anticipate and to take action ahead of time to avoid it becoming depression.

– Gia, 25.

I always have a headache if I'm late, even if I meet someone who's always late. A few years ago, in a group therapy session, a teacher who always asked everyone to be on time gave me a task to be 10 to 15 minutes late. He knew I wouldn't do it. Every time I have a scheduled day, it's in my head. I feel very anxious if I don't follow the schedule until I realize that certain things can be done tomorrow or that I could even ask others for help in doing them. I really become very outraged when I think 'I have to do everything around me'—then I realize that the only person who is demanding is myself.

- Violette, 56.

I feel so tense and serious. Inside, I feel a constant feeling that everything has to be in its place and done right. And it doesn't matter what it is: a party, a conversation, a trip, a presentation, or even the way a room is displayed. I can be quite a difficult personality, often voicing my opinion toward others in various situations, such as seeing a teacher giving incomplete or not entirely correct information. Everything must be done correctly, according to priorities. At some point, I was proud of having this view, but more and more often I start to feel tired of asking so much of myself.

– Caroline, 25.

I constantly feel overwhelmed by a desire to do just the right thing in every situation—to control my feelings and thoughts so that they don't slip out into the view of others; and if they accidentally get out, I try to express them in the right way. I constantly feel anger inside; and the more I experience that feeling, the more I judge myself that it is not good to feel this way and that I am a bad person. I am already aware of my problem and I am trying to practice observing my feelings to see where they are coming from. I ask myself often: 'What truly makes me angry in this situation?' You would be surprised at what I sometimes discover.

– Thomas, 30.

Now I can see and understand my meaningless internal criticism. That difficult feeling, when every time everything is not okay. Everything could be better. When there is no harmony inside and no limits for the word 'better'. But the funniest thing is that no one actually criticizes me except myself. The only person supposed to love me was me, but I was the last one in the world to do that. Of course, I cannot complain that this way of thinking opens a lot of doors for me and gives me a lot of work opportunities, but the peace I experience now truly cannot be better than any money or opportunities. Now I do what I can do the best, and when something is wrong I accept it; that is a part of life where we need to learn. Overall, perfection is a very subjective thing. I often ask myself if anyone can actually be perfect except God.

– Felicity, 42.

Do you
know when I started to feel
free? When the realization finally came to me
that, no matter how much I believed that I was doing
what I really wanted in life, I truly wasn't. I thought that all of
my decisions were free, and that was what I wanted. I had a few
friends who seemed 'weak' to me, who often repeated that I was thinking
too logically and making decisions without listening to my heart. Of course,
I didn't believe them, but as I walked through life I always faced the same
feedback, just from different people, until I finally realized that there were a lot of
things in my heart that I wouldn't think of doing because of fear of being judged
by others. I would find logical justifications about why one action or the other
would be wrong to act on. Although I'm still finding myself a little bit hesitant to
act on some things, my heart's decisions take priority now. The judgment from
others is only opinion, they judge themselves —not me. I am free to choose,
regardless of the opinion of others.

— *Abby, 29.*

In my opinion, it is very important that we, the inhabitants of the Earth, nurture and care
for our nature. I actually feel very upset inside when I see people who use more than they
truly need. I remember once my whole family planned to go for a picnic. We all gathered
and we planned to spend the whole day out in nature. When planning what I should bring
along, I thought carefully and decided to take plates from the house that I could wash and
reuse. When everyone gathered at the table, everyone except my husband and me were
using plastic plates. I could not refrain from expressing my opinion on their reckless use
of plastic plates, which caused a conflict in the family and my brother shouted, 'What's the
difference to you in how we live? Maybe it seems to help you, but what if I believe that using
water to clean your plates is worse for the environment? Let us live in the way we want.'
In the moment I was upset at him, but now I realize that sometimes I follow my truth too
obsessively, believing that it is better.

— *Thelma, 38.*

Revealing myself

———

Tips for personal awareness

Thoughts encouraging growth

40 daily exercises

Bringing awareness to yourself

By becoming aware of your day-to-day behavior, you gain the ability to respond to situations in the way that you truly want to. Take a good look at the following recommendations which were created specifically for your type. Expand your awareness by integrating them into your daily practices.

⟨ ◈ ⟩

◇

Practice prioritizing your personal desires and dreams, even if they seem illogical or inconsistent with other expectations.

◇

Notice when you are experiencing one feeling, but outwardly expressing something different to your surroundings.

◇

Pay attention when you internally start to criticize yourself. Is that criticism real or does it only appear because you do not meet your invented standards? Take several deep breaths and release. You are good and enough.

◇

Practice seeing the goodness in where you are. Asking yourself: What is right about this moment? Without taking responsibility to change anything, how can I best engage in what is happening here and now?

◇

Practice accepting your fear of not being good or right.

◇

Pay attention when you begin to justify your actions to others.

 Allow yourself to act as you wish, as often as possible—not as you should act according to set norms.

 Take as much time as possible for types of relaxation which have no goals: spending time with friends, playing games, spending time in nature, etc.

 Notice when you instinctively start to judge yourself or others. Take the time to think about this trait: whether it is you or whether it is a recurring habit that is within you. Accept this feeling and let go, replacing it with a positive thought.

 Pay attention when you take on work or do the right thing in order to be good, but not because that would be your true want/wish.

 Take time for practices that awaken inner love and compassion for yourself.

 Notice when you start correcting others and instructing others on how they should live. Grow within yourself the awareness that others have the right to choose to live as they wish.

 Notice when you start worrying about decisions that are based on the fear of being wrong.

 As soon as you hear the criticism inside, stop for a minute and ask yourself, "Is it really so bad?"

 Observe your fear of being a bad person who has flaws; and also when you subconsciously begin to feel that making mistakes is bad.

Thoughts
Encouraging Growth

Every thought has the potential to take your life in a new direction. The following messages were carefully selected for your Enneagram type. Take some time to read each message and consider how you can incorporate them into your daily life.

◇ **Practice** seeing that everyone is inherently valuable.

◇ **Appreciate** every perspective—there is more than one way to live.

◇ **Consider the thought** that perhaps there is nothing in this world which needs to be corrected or improved. There may be a possibility that everything is perfect as it is.

◇ **Focusing on the good** sides of your personality will awaken a sense of gratitude within you.

◇ **Accept** your own and others' imperfections.

◇ **Take more time** for yourself: personal development, relaxation, entertainment.

◇ **Learn to see** perfection in what surrounds you here and now.

◇ **Stop for a moment** and do what you really want instead.

◇ **Discover** for yourself that existence of differences is a natural part of life and of personal growth and change.

◇ **Find out** what you are not allowing for yourself because of your judgment of others.

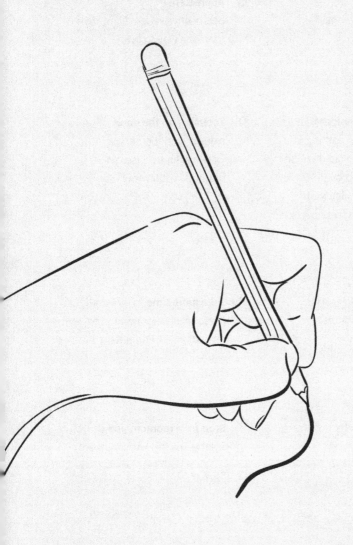

Daily
exercises
for personal growth

To follow these exercises is crucial. They were designed specifically for your type and they all lead to personal growth and free you from unwanted habits. Sometimes these exercises can look pointless, but trust that they form a bigger picture. Our personalities also tend to resist personal growth as a way to protect what is familiar, but in order to expand our understanding of ourselves, we need to go beyond what we already know and there is always something new to be learned. Youaremoreworld team is together with you on this personal journey. Just remember that there are so many people travelling the same path as you and they can already confirm the benefits of all the exercises.

Take one exercise per day.

1.

When you notice that you are judging yourself or others, stop for a moment and feel it. Is this really your true feeling? Maybe it's an automatically formed habit? This time can your heart choose compassion instead of judgment? What is more beneficial in your opinion?

Write your notes here

Today is a day for yourself only. If there are situations where you need to give up things for others that are important to you, keep at least one thing you will do for yourself today. At the end of the day, write for yourself; how does it feel to intentionally do things for yourself? Why do you think it feels this way?

Write your notes here

3.

Share your feelings with close friends. What feelings do you experience? Notice how difficult it is to share your feelings. If it is difficult, then ask yourself why it is so. What are you going through? The people of your type often tend to rationalize their feelings because they feel afraid of being criticized or judged by others.

Write your notes here

How do you decide when you are a good person? What criteria must you meet? Can others meet the same criteria to become good people as well? Describe your picture of "a good person." Will you always be good to everyone by living by this definition?

Write your notes here

5.

What is true connection with another person? Is it based on mutual understanding and caring? Look around your environment; think about whether the relationships you maintain are the way you truly want. If not, what is missing to satisfy you? What can you do today to make a difference?

Write your notes here

Pay attention when you experience anxiety inside yourself about possible criticism from others. What do you have to give up in the moment to avoid it? Who suffers the most? How do you decide when you would receive criticism from others, and when you will be supported by others?

Write your notes here

7.

Today, begin by writing a list of things you would like to do for yourself in the space provided below. When other people's needs arise, try to remember to consider your own priorities. Bring the focus back to personal agreement with yourself and what your heart truly wants for your personal well-being. Your needs are just as important as others', and unfortunately no one will look after them if you don't take personal responsibility for them. Speak with the others, perhaps their needs can wait and you can meet your own needs first.

Write your notes here

Accept that you might be defined as a bad person by someone, but that doesn't indicate your personal value. Every person has different values and different ways in which they value their surroundings, which is really personal and does not have much to do with your personality. How does it make you feel to know that someone considers you to be a bad person? Write down your thoughts below:

Write your notes here

9.

Score from 1 to 10 the love you have toward yourself. What do you love yourself for? Can the opinions of others affect this feeling? If yes, why is it so?

Write your notes here

Allow yourself to accept your own and others' imperfections. We all try to be the best people we can be in the moment. If you see how your advice could help others, try to formulate it without being too specific or direct as this can come across as a command. Advice given out of love always touches the heart; but if we give it only because we think that we know better, we are met with the other person's self-defence. Try this method and see if you receive different responses from others. Write down what differences you notice in the response of others when you share your advice from the heart without seeking to change them, by simply helping them to cope better with their situation.

Write your notes here

11.

Write down the standards you are aware that you are following (for example: always eat before six, always respond to a message once you receive one, etc. It could be anything you consider to be a repeatable action). Share them with someone close to you, see if they are valid and important to the other person. Listen with awareness to hear different perspectives, they are not judging you; they are simply sharing their personal preference. Ask yourself a simple question: Does the whole world follow the same standards as you follow, or does everyone have their own?

Write your notes here

Consider the thought that perhaps there is nothing in this world that you need to correct or improve, that everything is perfect as it is. Close your eyes and allow yourself to have this thought. How does it feel for you? What feelings arise inside you?

Write your notes here

13.

Ask how much your inner standards help you, and how much they hinder you. Who creates them? Consider 5 positive things you notice from living by them, and 5 things which you see as a limitation of them.

Write your notes here

Notice how many times a day you feel frustrated by the actions or decisions of others. Keep a personal journal where you can mark your notes every time you feel frustrated. By what standards do you evaluate them? What value do they give you?

Write your notes here

At what point do you become overwhelmed or upset about the plans you have set for yourself? Stop and ask yourself: Why are you seeking to achieve one goal or another? Who/what is this important for? Is this frustration you are experiencing worth the goal you are trying to achieve? Pay special attention to the internal dialogue you experience within yourself. What do you tell yourself?

Write your notes here

As an exercise, try writing down 7 statements which you do not believe, for example; "hunting is a great thing to do", or anything else which goes against your values. Try to write down 10 positive sentences for each of the 7 statements. Which aspects of this exercise did you find positive for yourself? How does this change your understanding of the topics which you were originally against?

Write your notes here

17.

Today, focus and observe how often you judge yourself for behavior where you deemed that you were not enough. Catch yourself in the moment and transfer your focus to conscious breathing. What is it that you do well in this situation for which you can thank yourself? Do other people in this situation value you in the same way that you do? Repeat to yourself several times, "I love myself no matter what I do."

Write your notes here

Set aside one day a week when you have no responsibilities after work or on the weekend, and allow time for yourself. Note that there must be no achievements, no expectations, no requirements in the activity you choose to do for yourself. Is it easy for you to stay in such activities? Why?

Write your notes here

19.

Practice gratitude this week. Take five minutes in the evening and think about all the things which have happened today. Find at least 10 things you can be thankful for today. If it is more convenient for you, you can write them down. It is very important that you notice things you can thank yourself for. Maybe you listened to a random stranger when he needed you. Maybe you did someone a favour even though you had a lot of work to do. These are just a couple of examples. What is your list of things you are grateful for?

Write your notes here

20.

"I have a mission in life." How does it feel to "have a mission"? What do you want to achieve with it? How do you express this "feeling of having a mission" outwardly?

21.

"I know how things have to be done." Read this sentence a couple times and take some time to explore what the word *"know"* means for you in this context. What makes you feel so sure about knowing? How do you know that it is done in the correct way? How do you measure this?

Write your notes here

Ask someone who is close to you for help solving a problem or completing a task (family, colleague, teacher etc). Try this exercise even if you do not specifically have a need for assistance. How do you feel asking for help? Is it easy for you to trust others to do a good job? Why is that?

Write your notes here

23.

Score from 1 to 10 how often you criticize yourself during the day (1 being very little and 10 being a lot). Also score how often you show love to yourself in the same way. What do these results tell you? Does this result encourage you to take some new actions?

Write your notes here

Review your schedule for this week. Are there at least 3 things this week you have decided to do just for yourself? Do you devote enough time to rest? Are you eating properly? Do you engage in activities that you enjoy?

Write your notes here

25.

When giving feedback to others, be sure to start with what is positive about a specific thing or situation. Sometimes it seems in your mind that certain things have to be naturally understood and are not worth talking about, but no one can read your thoughts. Everyone is sensitive to criticism, help others feel valued and be seen—even for the smallest things they do.

Write your notes here

It is common for you to give up your personal desires in order to remain good in the eyes of others. Notice every moment of this week when you choose to be good. What can you see in common in all of these situations? Notice how often your behavior is determined in this way. How much do you have to give up for the image of being a "good" person?

Write your notes here

27.

Write a short text on the topic of harmony. What is harmony for you? How do you imagine it? How much harmony do you have in your life? Is it close to you? How often do you embrace it in your day?

Write your notes here

Catch yourself when you start doing things for others in order to be a good person. Ask yourself: can I be absolutely sure that if I don't take this action, the view that others have of me would change?

◇

29.

When we forgive ourselves, the forgiveness allows our inner peace. Allow yourself to practice forgiveness every day for a week. Try to spend at least a few minutes forgiving yourself for specific things, and forgive others who hurt you. Write down how you felt after each practice. Do you feel lighter? Do you still have the same difficult feeling? Write down what is happening inside you.

Write your notes here

Allow yourself to take a break this week from improving your surroundings. Practice shifting your focus from what aspects need to be improved to what is already good about them. Practice noticing what is good in each situation. Share with others what they did well, notice if you get either positive or negative feedback from them. How does it feel to evaluate what is already good and express that to others?

Write your notes here

31.

It is very important that when you feel angry inside, you share it with others—especially with those who are responsible for the emotion you experience. Learn to express it in peace, sharing in a beautiful form, how the behavior of the other has made you feel. To avoid situations in the future that prevent us from behaving kindly, we must share them with others. Most people don't even think about how their behavior will make you feel, be open to yourself and others. Sharing does not make you a worse person.

Write your notes here

List 10 situations where you experience personal criticism. Take the time to think about them, and ask yourself what all of those situations have in common.

Write your notes here

33.

Write down all of the judgmental thoughts you have experienced today. "How do I judge myself? How do I decide what is right, wrong, good or bad? How does the critic inside me make me feel? What is "right" at this moment?"

Write your notes here

Write down 20 things you love about yourself. Read them aloud to yourself. Feel the heat which, like radiating energy, moves through your body. How often do you experience this energy during the day?

Write your notes here

Each person completes any given task to the best of their abilities. Each person has uniqueness, and by embracing our differences we can help each other to grow. Share your work and responsibilities with others. Notice what you can learn from others. How often do you admit that the way others complete a task is more correct than your own way? Do you see the truth in other people's opinions? Do you respectfully manage to hear different opinions?

Write your notes here

Notice how often you experience a feeling that you have to justify yourself to others. What situations make you feel this way? Do others demand excuses from you in a given situation? Why is it important to justify yourself to others? What does this give to you? What are you trying to defend?

Write your notes here

37.

Catch yourself as you begin to moralize or explain to others how they need to live, notice if this gives positive emotions to them. Do you see other ways you could communicate the same information differently? If you get a negative reaction, be sure to share the intention you had; expand the content and give them more information. Practice giving your advice with helpful and honest intentions.

Write your notes here

Perfectionism is a word that is understood by everyone differently. Write down 10 sentences about what perfection is for you. Why is it so important for you?

Write your notes here

39.

"I accept different people and their perceptions." Why is it important to hear a different perspective? How do you appreciate and accept that perspective? Do you feel like you are interested in something new about the world, or is it beneficial for you? If not, why is it so? Do you feel like one perspective is better than the other?

Write your notes here

❝❝

A day spent judging another is a painful day.
A day spent judging yourself is also a painful day.

Buddha

Today is a positive affirmation day. Choose one or two affirmations and repeat them in your mind or out loud throughout your day. Write down what shift of your mindset you may have noticed and which thoughts have appeared when you say the affirmations.

Write your notes here

AFFIRMATIONS:
I am perfect even in all my imperfections.
I accept who I am.
I am at ease with life.
I forgive myself and others.
I set reasonable expectations for myself.
I choose to focus my attention on what is going right in my life.
I choose to be kind, compassionate and understanding.
I accept that everyone is doing the best they can with whatever resources they have.
I learn to laugh at myself.
I love being and having fun!

Source: www.evelynlim.com

If you find it difficult working on your daily exercises by yourself, please join our community and discover the support it offers. Write us an email to learn more about programs that are available at this stage:
youaremoreworld@gmail.com

If you complete all of your daily exercises, please share your experience with us and be in the draw to win goods from our **Youaremoreworld shop.**

Notes

Notes

Notes

Accepting myself

Accepting all that I am

Making conscious choices

Letting go

Step 1

I accept that I sometimes judge others for not meeting my standards/ expectations.

I accept that sometimes when I feel angry, I avoid expressing my emotions and judge myself for feeling this way.

I accept that I can be very hard on myself when making even the smallest mistake.

Balanced sense of self-discipline

Self-supportive and self-loving

Honest

I accept that sometimes I have a hard time accepting that I am tired and need rest.

When I accept both sides of my personality, my strengths gain even more power

I accept that I often feel that I am not good enough.

Feel integrity from doing good

Treating others fairly

I accept that I can find it difficult to ask for help from others and to share my responsibilities.

I accept that I take a lot of responsibility, even for the lives of others.

Hopeful

Accepting

Reliable

Accepting myself

—————⟨◈⟩—————

There is no greater gift that we can give ourselves than that of true acceptance of who we are, seeing our whole self with an open heart. This allows us a sense of curiosity and braveness to see our faults as well as our gifts without casting judgment on them, simply able to observe ourselves as we are. It is in these moments that we are able to feel the truth of our existence arising, understanding that who we are now has a long history. Through our lives we are touched by each of our experiences, which forms the understanding we have of the world and shapes the unique expression we bring to the world. Each of these qualities — those that form the uniqueness we bring to the world — was born with a purpose of supporting us during a specific period of our life; however, we often resist these qualities. Perhaps this resistance is because we want to be different, or because those in our surroundings don't approve of these qualities. Whatever the reason, we all respond to these unwanted qualities in the same way: we abandon them, ignoring them as though they are not a part of us, until they become our shadows, limiting us and preventing us from living the best life we are truly meant to live.

The first step on the journey of our own healing is to accept that there is nothing wrong with the qualities we have which we consider as negative; they all have a purpose to serve. As we move through different periods of our lives, we require different qualities, and these eventually form the bigger picture of who we are; so our only task for now is to **accept this variety of qualities without judgment.**

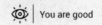

To start, **write a list of all of the qualities and traits** which are dominant to your personality that you consider to be negative. Make sure you add all of the qualities you can think of, especially those that you feel most uncomfortable about. Some examples of this could be: *sometimes I have a hard time accepting that I am tired and need rest;* or, *I often feel that I am not good enough.* Or you can simply write a quality, like being stubborn or often feeling jealous (you can find more examples in *picture 1*). We recommend being as specific as you can, remembering situations where you experienced the qualities on your list, for example: *I feel jealous when others are more successful than me.* You may want to use some of the new knowledge you have gained from this book to support you in writing this list. If you feel some resistance or hesitation toward certain qualities, add them to the list as well. Often the qualities that we strongly resist make up a shadow side of ourselves.

Once you have written the list of qualities, take some time to go over the examples and see if any of those qualities resonate with you. If so, add them to your list. When you are all done, move on to the second part of this exercise — "Accepting all that I am".

Balanced sense
of self-discipline

Honest

Treating
others fairly

Feel integrity
from doing good

Accepting

Reliable

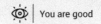

For this step, simply go through your list of descriptions of qualities one by one and add **"I accept that..."** before each description. Take time to sit with each quality to feel this acceptance. For example, *"I accept that sometimes I can be very hard on myself when making even the smallest mistake. And now I am conscious of it." "I accept that I sometimes judge others for not meeting my standards."* etc.

Accepting all that I am

Bringing our shadow side to the light

I accept that *I can be very hard on myself when making even the smallest mistake. And now I am conscious of it.*

Step 2

Making conscious choices

Once you have taken time to accept your different qualities, you may notice that some of them contradict what you currently value in your life and that some of the qualities are no longer valuable for you. This is a very natural state for us as humans because it is in our nature to constantly grow and change. The ability to look into our hearts with honesty and to see our whole selves, including all of our practiced personality traits, allows us to experience a sense of empowerment and the inner strength to act on it.

In order to experience the change which we are seeking, it is important to embrace the positive aspects of the quality in order to align it with our true values. Use the following exercise to expand the positive aspects of your qualities:

I might .... but I choose to...

Take some time to fill-in the boxes below based on the qualities you discovered in the first step of this exercise.

I might *feel that I am not good enough.*

but I choose to *recognize and acknowledge all of the good things that I do for myself and others in every day*

I might

but I choose to

I might

but I choose to

I might

but I choose to

I might ....

but I choose to...

....

....

I might ....

....

but I choose to...

....

....

I might ....

....

but I choose to...

....

....

I might ....

....

but I choose to...

....

....

....

I might ....

....

but I choose to...

....

....

....

I might ....

....

but I choose to...

....

....

....

Step 3

Letting go

Following the exercise — "Accepting all that I am", you may find that you still hold a feeling of resistance toward some of your qualities. This is very natural, as many of our qualities have been with us for as long as we can remember. With this in mind, it is good to remain sensitive toward ourselves as we work through the exercises.

Use the following exercise to work with the qualities which you still feel some resistance toward:

I accept that my quality of _____

_____ has

been a part of who I am for a long time. I appreciate everything this quality has done for me up until now. Thank you for protecting me, thank you for giving me clarity in certain moments, thank you for guiding me through some challenging situations; my life has now changed and I release you with gratitude. My future plans require the new quality of _____

_____ and I lovingly

invite _____

_____ to be a part of who I am, starting from today. I know that as you are a new quality that it takes time for me to know you, to feel you and to understand how you manifest in my being. I ask you to help me to fulfill my future plans and to support the continuation of my unique journey. This month, I will use all of my effort to express you in any moment that I am able to. I will accept you as part of my identity and from this moment on I feel the benefit of this choice.

Each of our actions originates from our inner intention. When we want something different, we develop different qualities in order to get it. Within Enneagram, each of the types also comes from a similar origin of developing qualities from a basis of inner intention.

Having completed the deep inner work leading up to this point, we can now move on to the final exercise: Identifying with your future self.

Healing myself

Identifying with your future self

Healing yourself

Revealing yourself

Meditation

Affirmations for aligning with your true self

Within a year from today I will:

I commit to doing the following to create the quality life I deserve to live:

Identifying with your future self

The knowledge of Enneagram is not about simply putting us into a box; it is a valuable tool that can show us that we are living a limited version of ourselves and that we have the potential to be much more — that there is a way out of that box. The moment we accept what we learn about the qualities of our dominant type, we gain the freedom to expand our qualities and to become whatever we want. We will still hold the basis of our dominant type, as this is our gift which supports our soul on this journey. However, as we appreciate ourselves as we are, we are able to see which traits are limiting us and integrate more positive qualities to support us in realizing our dreams. Take some time today to consider **who you would like to become by the end of this year.** How would you like your life to look? Which qualities would you like to have? What goals would you have accomplished? You might also consider your relationship, health and finances etc. Be as specific as you can and take your time in writing it all down. If you aren't able to finish this exercise in one sitting, simply return to it when you feel ready to explore your expanded future.

Once you have written all of your wishes, take this piece of paper and put it somewhere visible where you will see it often. Take 5 minutes every day to imagine how it will feel to live this life that you want to live. The more time you take to imagine your future self, the more information you are providing for your subconscious to direct your actions in your desired direction. Sooner than you might expect you will notice that you are already acting with the traits you had on your wish list. For example, if you write on your list that you would like to be an engaging person when you are with others, you will notice that you begin to experience more frequent possibilities for you to express this quality. If, on your list, you had a specific workplace noted, you will find yourself guided to more direct actions toward realizing this.

In our lives, we always have the choice, to either be directed by unconscious actions or to be proactive in learning about ourselves and building the life that we truly want to live. This leads us to realize that there is much more to Enneagram than simply being one of the types; it can guide us to be more and to live honestly through each new moment that unfolds for us.

Healing yourself

The things to which we are exposed every day become our reality. When practiced often, the sentences below have the potential to bring you into greater alignment with your heart.

Affirmation:
I am complete
when I celebrate my
imperfections.

Confession:
I accept what is, as it is,
starting with my perfect
and flawed self.

Expand your awareness

Healing:
Maybe others are right. Maybe someone else has a better idea.
Maybe others will learn for themselves.
Maybe I've done all that can be done.

*"Because true belonging only happens when we
present our authentic, imperfect selves to the world,
our sense of belonging can never be greater than
our level of self-acceptance."*

Brené Brown

Revealing yourself

The following questions have been created uniquely for your type, offering new perspectives for you to consider about yourself. Take some time to give thought to each question individually, and write your thoughts below.

———————————— ⟨ ◈ ⟩ ————————————

In what ways do I find myself condemning or **judging myself?**

_____

_____

_____

What criteria do I use to determine whether a situation is **good or bad, right or wrong?**

_____

_____

_____

In what ways do I **measure myself against others?**

_____

_____

How do I define **what is "right"?**

_____

_____

How does it make me feel when I **criticize myself?**

_____

_____

_____

_____

_____

_____

Meditation
for your daily practise

 It takes 5- 10 min.

Find a peaceful, secure place,
close your eyes and repeat the sentences below:

Notice how, with each sentence, your heart begins
to open up, allowing you to feel stronger in your
own body. Feel how this process awakens the
true understanding of yourself, which has always
existed within.

May I be at ease.
May I breathe peacefully
May I find freedom in rest

By Christopher L. Heuertz

Practicing self-acceptance and unravelling our beliefs helps us to see ourselves more fully. This awakens a new sense of knowing within us, despite the occasional thoughts that make us feel smaller. Consider the following sentences and how they represent a deep inner truth you have always known:

When I free myself
I would gain the knowledge that:

⟨ ◈ ⟩

I can allow myself to relax and enjoy life;

the best I can do is good enough;

I am grateful that others have many things to teach me;

I can make mistakes without condemning myself;

my feelings are legitimate and that I have a right to feel them;

I treat others with tenderness and respect;

I am gentle and forgiving of myself;

I am compassionate and forgiving of others;

life is good and unfolding in miraculous ways.

Source: Don Richard Riso, Enneagram Transformations.
Houghton Mifflin Company, 1993, 129 pages.

Additional exercises
supporting your personal growth

How I want my future to look

Making balanced decisions based on the 9 perspectives of Enneagram

Expanding my beliefs with Byron Katie's 4 question technique

"The goal is not to be better than the other man, but your previous self."

Dalai Lama XIV

How I want my future to look

As humans, it is common for us to focus specifically on one single thing when it comes to planning (improve a relationship, change career, etc.). One of the keys for true happiness is to keep balance across all of the important areas of our life. Take some time to think about the areas listed below, and consider what would you like to achieve in each within the coming year. Write down all of the ideas that come to you. Take some time to act toward your priorities, as this can add great value to your overall well-being.

⟨ ◈ ⟩

Personal development

For example: read three books about self-love.

For example: spend more time with my mother.

Relationships

Career

For example: ask for X responsibility that would help toward moving into a team leader position.

Leisure

For example: take a day trip to X town.

Home

For example: change the tiles in my bathroom.

Finances

For example: transfer 10% from my salary into a savings account.

◇

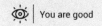

Making balanced decisions
based on the 9 perspectives of Enneagram

Making decisions can be an overwhelming experience, especially when we are not sure which of the options would be the right one for the outcome we are seeking. Take some time to review a situation in your life that requires a decision by using the 9 questions offered below, each of which represents one of the 9 Enneagram types:

---

1. What exactly do I not like in this situation?

2. For whom will it be beneficial if I change this situation?

3. Which end-result am I reaching for, and when does it have to be done?

4. How can I solve this situation by using my creativity?

5. What information am I still missing?

6. What kind of danger could I face while I am solving this situation?

7. What are possible solutions for this situation?

8. What is an action plan?

9. How will I reward myself when I finish?

Expanding my beliefs
with Byron Katie's 4 question technique

────────────────< ◈ >────────────────

Byron Katie's work has had an incredible impact on many people, helping them to better understand their thoughts and to increase their well-being. She created a 4-question system, where by going through each question, we can discover how many of our thoughts are based on false stories which repeatedly cause stress and anxiety. Once we become comfortable questioning our thoughts, we can use this exercise to work with our underlying beliefs which are no longer relevant for our reality.

We added this technique to the book alongside the knowledge of Enneagram, because we can see how much it can help those who want to take their path of inner work into their own hands.

Byron Katie's 4-question technique:

1. Is it true?
2. Can you absolutely know that it's true?
3. How do you react, what happens, when
   you believe that thought?
4. Who would you be without that thought?

Underlying belief:

"I have to be good and then I will be loved."

## STEP 1	## STEP 2

Let's question this belief using Byron Katie's four-question technique.

1. Is it true that you have to be good to be loved by others?

- Yes

2. Can you absolutely be sure that you have to be good to be loved by others?

- No

3. How do you feel/react when you think that you have to be good to be loved?

   - I feel like I can't make any mistakes. I have to be right. Then I feel angry because I can't fully be myself.

4. Who would you be without this thought that you have to be good to be loved by others?

   - I would not think too much about which action is good or bad, I would just act how it feels in the moment and never blame myself for not being perfect.

Looking at the belief from three different perspectives.

Turn it around to yourself
I have to love myself. This is my job.

Turn it around to the others
*I have to love others even
if they are not good.*

Turn it around to the opposite
*I do not need to be good
to be loved by others.
(They either choose to love me
or not, for who I truly am)*

*Note: the answers are included simply
as an example. Follow your own
thoughts and discover the answers
which are true for you.*

If you would like further support in understanding this technique, please see Byron Katie's website or her many valuable books.

Bibliography

1. Baron Renee Baron and Wagele Elizabeth. The Enneagram made easy: Discover the 9 types of people. New York, 1994.

2. Ford, Debbie. The Dark Side of the Light Chasers. USA, 1998.

3. Heuertz, Christopher L. The Enneagram of Belonging: A Compassionate Journey of Self –Acceptance. Grand Rapids, MI: Zondervan, 2020.

4. Riso, Don Richard, and Russ Hudson. The Wisdom of the Enneagram: The Complete Guide to Psychological and Spiritual Growth for the Nine Personality Types. New York: Bantam, 1999.

5. "Revealing yourself" source of information: www.enneagramworldwide.com

Recommended books

1. *You Can Heal Your Life* by Louise L. Hay

2. *The Power of Now* by Eckhart Tolle

3. *The Gifts of Imperfection* by Brené Brown

4. *The Dance of Anger* by Harriet Lerner

5. *Compassion* by Osho

6. *The Dark Side of the Light Chasers* by Ford Debbie

7. *The Artist's Way* by Julia Cameron

8. *The Power of Positive Thinking* by Norman Vincent Peale

9. *Big Magic: Creative living beyond fear* by Elizabeth Gilbert

10. *The Mindful Path to Self Compassion* by Christopher Germer

11. *Wabi Sabi* by Beth Kempton

12. *The 5 Love Languages: The Secret to Love That Lasts* by Gary Chapman

13. *Emotional Intelligence: Why It Can Matter More Than IQ* by Daniel Goleman

14. *Loving what is* by Byron Katie

15. *Intuition* by Osho

16. *The Wisdom of the Enneagram* by Don Richard Riso and Russ Hudson

17. *The Enneagram of Belonging* by Christopher L. Heuertz

18. *The Enneagram made easy* by Renee Baron & Elizabeth Wagele

19. *The Untethered Soul: The Journey Beyond Yourself* by Michael Alan Singer

20. *Why Won't You Apologize?* Harriet Lerner

◇

Who are we?

Youaremoreworld was built on an idea to encourage others to their own personal growth. Our mission is to awaken curiosity in people, helping them to learn more about themselves, questioning their beliefs - especially the ones which no longer serve them. Encouraging their sense of freedom in order to allow them to live what truly matters to them. For all of us, our origin is the same, having been conditioned and trained by our surroundings, however, we all also equally have the opportunity to reconnect to our true selves and to release what's no longer needed. Enneagram is an incredibly valuable resource to begin this process. Here at *Youaremoreworld*, we use the knowledge of Enneagram as the basis for our work, helping people to uncover the "persona" which they have formed in order to interact with daily life.

The Enneagram exercise book you have in your hands is one of a collection of nine books, each serving a different Enneagram type. We hope that this book will serve its purpose and assist you in your further journey of self-discovery.

We are constantly expanding the horizons here at *Youaremoreworld*, seeking new ways in which we can serve the greater community. If you liked our book, please join us at **www.youaremoreworld.com** and stay up to date with the work we are doing. The greatest gift we can receive is your feedback to help us to continually improve.

Thank you for being a part of our community, we will see you out there in the wilderness, where your heart directs the footsteps of your unique soul.

With Gratitude,
Viltare and Simona

Contact us:

✉ youaremoreworld@gmail.com

✈ www.youaremoreworld.com

🅕 youaremore_world

🅞 youaremore_world

Read
with us

Learn
with us

Shop
with us

Books
in this collection

Acknowledgements

Only with the help of others we can reach the stars

Thank you to our teachers Don Richard Riso and Russ Hudson who compiled all of the knowledge of Enneagram and inspired many people around the world to look into their hearts and unlock their own potential. They were also a great inspiration for us to publish these exercise books for anyone who chooses Enneagram as a tool for their own personal growth.

We would love to give credit to Christopher L. Heuertz for his talent of approaching the Enneagram with great compassion, encouraging others to accept the full spectrum of their personality (including the sides which may be viewed as incompetence or limitation). You will find his meditations, affirmations and confessions which, when practiced daily, can heal the heart.

Also, we would like to acknowledge Jack Labanauskas for his constant work in keeping the Enneagram community alive and connected through his "Enneagram monthly" magazine which can be joined by visiting:
http://www.enneagram-monthly.com/

Our superstar Matthew Fulton, who reviewed each page with the most sincere eye, making sure that every word would be written in a correct and most understandable way. You are part of Youaremoreworld family, thank you for your hard work.

We are very grateful for our parents: Viltare's (Leonora and Virginijus, and the best grandma in the world Antanina) and Simona's (Lijana and Rimgaudas) for giving us the freedom to explore this life and for providing support in all of its possible forms. We are also grateful for our partners Hanno and Dan for providing us with inspiration and encouragement through all of the steps required to publish all our work. And lastly our Enneagram teacher Nadezda Doronina-Koltan, who opened the door for us to discover this great wisdom and to guide us to the master class of understanding.

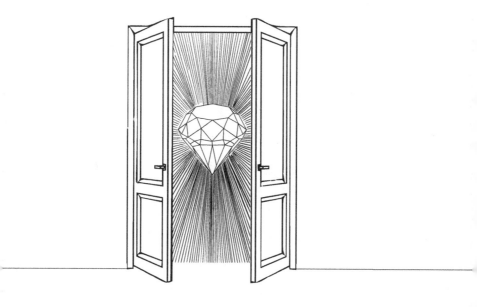

Made in the USA
Las Vegas, NV
12 December 2024

14034782R00075